Read-About® Geography

Japan

By David F. Marx

Consultant
Linda Cornwell, Learning Resource Consultant,
Indiana Department of Education

CP Children's Press®
A Division of Grolier Publishing
New York   London   Hong Kong   Sydney
Danbury, Connecticut

Visit Children's Press® on the Internet at:
http://publishing.grolier.com

Designer: Herman Adler Design Group

Library of Congress Cataloging-in-Publication Data

Marx, David F.
    Japan / by David F. Marx; consultant, Linda Cornwell.
      p. cm. – (Rookie read-about geography)
    Includes index.
    Summary: An introduction to the geography, people, and culture of
Japan, a nation comprised of many islands.
    ISBN 0-516-21551-5 (lib. bdg.)   0-516-26793-0 (pbk.)
    1. Japan—Juvenile literature. [1. Japan.] I. Cornwell, Linda.
II. Title. III. Series.
DS806.M379   1999
952—dc21

99-10670
CIP

Japan is a country on the continent of Asia. It is made up of many islands, large and small. People who live in Japan are called "Japanese." That is also the name of the language spoken in Japan.

Japanese students

A crowded neighborhood on the island of Honshu

Japan has four large islands where most people live. Their names are Hokkaido, Honshu, Shikoku, and Kyushu.

Not many people live on the hundreds of smaller islands that are also part of Japan. Some are too tiny to build a house on!

Japan is surrounded by water. To the west is the Sea of Japan. To the east is the big Pacific Ocean.

Sea of Japan

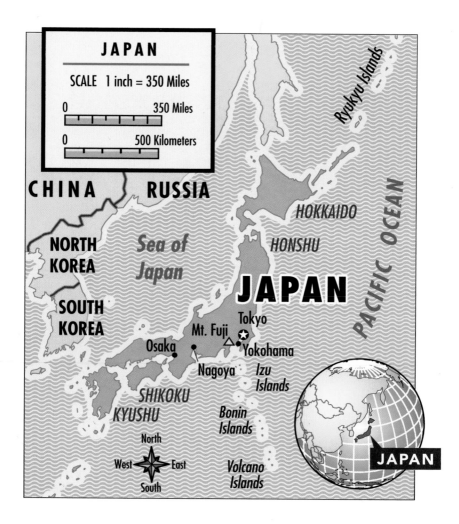

JAPAN

SCALE 1 inch = 350 Miles

0   350 Miles

0   500 Kilometers

CHINA   RUSSIA

NORTH
KOREA   HOKKAIDO

Sea of   HONSHU
Japan

JAPAN

SOUTH
KOREA   Tokyo
                 Mt. Fuji
        Osaka   Yokohama
                 Nagoya   Izu
                           Islands
    SHIKOKU
KYUSHU   Bonin
                  Islands
        North

West ✦ East

        South   Volcano
                    Islands

Ryukyu Islands

PACIFIC OCEAN

JAPAN

8

If you sail east across
the Pacific Ocean, you'll
reach California in the
United States.

To the west, across the
Sea of Japan, are Japan's
neighbor countries: South
Korea, North Korea,
China, and Russia.

Tokyo, the capital of Japan, is on the island of Honshu.

It is home to more than eight million people.

Tokyo, the capital of Japan

Tokyo's sidewalks are usually crowded with people.

Tokyo is an exciting, crowded city. From Tokyo, you can see the Pacific Ocean to the east and Mount Fuji to the west.

Mount Fuji is the tallest
of Japan's many mountains.
Its peak, or top, is 12,338
feet above the sea.

Mt. Fuji

A view of Osaka, Japan

Most of Japan's 123 million people live in Tokyo and other big cities.

These include Yokohama, Osaka, and Nagoya.

Many people who live
in these cities work in
businesses such as stores,
banks, and factories.

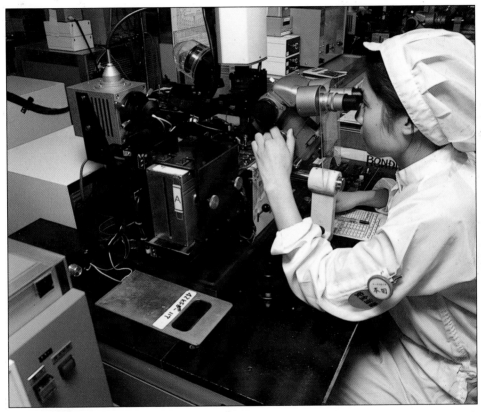

A worker in an electronics factory

One of Japan's car factories

Cars, computers, and televisions made in Japan are used by people all over the world.

Japanese people earn a
living in other ways, too.

Living on the seacoast,
many people catch and
sell fish and seaweed.
These are important
foods in Japan.

Japanese fishermen

Farmers at work in rice paddies

Living along rivers, farmers grow rice in soggy rice paddies.

In Japan, rice is eaten with almost every meal.

Living near mountains, some people work in mines. These people dig useful rocks out of the ground.

A Japanese worker in a coal mine

Japanese people have
learned to live in a place
where the land meets
the water, and where the
mountains reach to the sky.

Words You Know

factory

Japanese

mine

Mount Fuji

Osaka

rice paddies

Sea of Japan

Tokyo

31

Index

About the Author

David F. Marx is an author and editor of children's books.
He resides in Connecticut.

Photo Credits

Photographs ©: Cameramann Int'l Ltd.: 3, 11 left, 15 top, 19, 23, 30 top right, 30 bottom right, 31 bottom right, 12; H. Armstrong Roberts, Inc.: cover (A. Tovy), 16, 31 top left (Catherine Ursillo); International Stock Photo: 7, 31 bottom left (Chad Ehlers); Kyodo News International, Inc.: 27, 30 bottom left; National Geographic Image Collection: 24, 31 top right (George Moorey); Tony Stone Images: 20, 30 top left (Chad Ehlers), 28 (Gavin Hellier); Woodfin Camp & Associates: 4 (Mike Yamashita).
Map by Joe LeMonnier.